A Beginning-to-Read Book

T0082185

WHERE ANIMALS LIVE

by Mary Lindeen

NORWOOD HOUSE PRESS

DEAR CAREGIVER, The *Beginning to Read—Read and Discover Science* books provide young readers the opportunity to learn about scientific concepts while simultaneously building early reading skills. Each title corresponds to three of the key domains within the Next Generation Science Standards (NGSS): physical sciences, life sciences, and earth and space sciences.

The NGSS include standards that are comprised of three dimensions: Crosscutting Concepts, Science and Engineering Practices, and Disciplinary Core Ideas. The texts within the *Read and Discover Science* series focus primarily upon the Disciplinary Core Ideas and Crosscutting Concepts—helping readers view their world through a scientific lens. They pique a young reader's curiosity and encourage them to inquire and explore. The Connecting Concepts section at the back of each book offers resources to continue that exploration. The reinforcement activities at the back of the book support Science and Engineering Practices—to understand how scientists investigate phenomena in that world.

These easy-to-read informational texts make the scientific concepts accessible to young readers and prompt them to consider the role of science in their world. On one hand, these titles can develop background knowledge for exploring new topics. Alternately, they can be used to investigate, explain, and expand the findings of one's own inquiry. As you read with your child, encourage her or him to "observe"—taking notice of the images and information to formulate both questions and responses about what, how, and why something is happening.

Above all, the most important part of the reading experience is to have fun and enjoy it!

Sincerely,

Shannon Cannon

Shannon Cannon, PhD
Literacy Consultant

Norwood House Press
For more information about Norwood House Press please visit our website at www.norwoodhousepress.com or call 866-565-2900.
© 2021 Norwood House Press. Beginning-to-Read™ is a trademark of Norwood House Press. All rights reserved. No part of this book may be reproduced or utilized in any form or by any means without written permission from the publisher.

Editor: Judy Kentor Schmauss   **Designer**: Sara Radka

Photo Credits: Getty Images: cover, 1, 4, 5, 6, 7, 10, 11, 12, 13, 14, 16, 18, 20, 21, 22, 23, 24, 26, 28, 29; Shutterstock: 3, 5, 6, 8, 9, 10, 12, 13, 14, 15, 17, 18, 19, 20, 22, 24, 25, 26, 27, 29

Library of Congress Cataloging-in-Publication Data
Names: Lindeen, Mary, author.
Title: Where animals live / by Mary Lindeen.
Description: Chicago : Norwood House Press, [2022] | Series: Beginning-to-read | Audience: Grades K-1 | Summary: "Earth is home to millions of animals. Featured animals include those from forest, desert, mountain, rain forest, prairie, freshwater, and saltwater habitats. Includes science and reading activities and a word list"— Provided by publisher.
Identifiers: LCCN 2021019798 (print) | LCCN 2021019799 (ebook) | ISBN 9781684508266 (hardcover) | ISBN 9781684046560 (paperback) | ISBN 9781684046621 (epub)
Subjects: LCSH: Habitat (Ecology)—Juvenile literature. | Animal ecology—Juvenile literature.
Classification: LCC QH541.14 .L54 2022 (print) | LCC QH541.14 (ebook) | DDC 577—dc23
LC record available at https://lccn.loc.gov/2021019798
LC ebook record available at https://lccn.loc.gov/2021019799

Hardcover ISBN: 978-1-68450-826-6   Paperback ISBN: 978-1-68404-656-0

The world is full of animals.
Each animal needs a place to live.

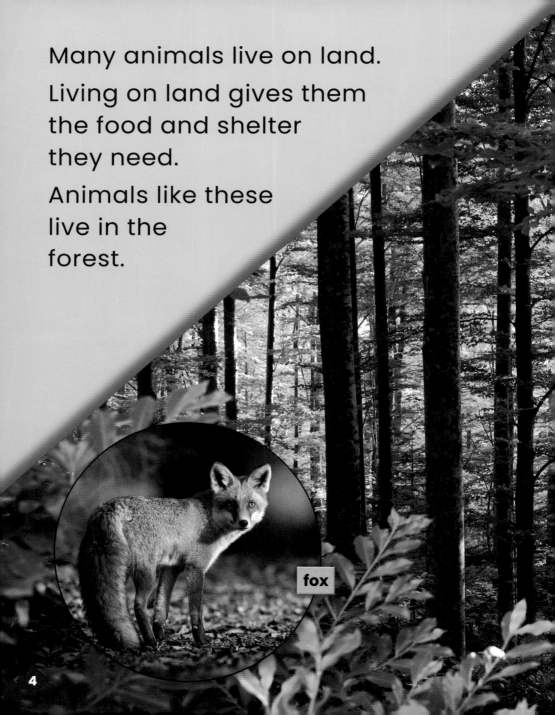

Many animals live on land. Living on land gives them the food and shelter they need.

Animals like these live in the forest.

fox

deer

bears

camels

lizard

Other animals live in the desert.

They can live where it is hot and dry.

meerkats

Some animals live in the mountains.

They can live where it is cool and rocky.

mountain goats

bighorn sheep

elk

9

toucan

monkey

These animals find the food and shelter they need in a rain forest.

Rain forests are warm and rainy places to live.

frog

Prairies have hot summers
and cold winters.

These animals live
on the prairie.

prairie dog

bison

coyote

fish

frog

14

Other animals live in the water.
Some need fresh water.
They live in lakes, rivers, and ponds.

duck

Other animals live in the ocean's salty water. Some of them live in coral reefs near the shore.

seahorse

sea turtle

clown fish

octopus

frogfish

Others live in the
deep sea.
The water is
dark and cold
there.

jellyfish

Animals like these travel all around the ocean. They can find food and shelter in many different places.

shark

whale

dolphin

It only takes a few months for hornets to build a nest the size of a basketball.

hornet's nest

spider

Some animals
build their own
homes.

beaver

bird

Other animals just find their homes.

fox

bear

raccoons

hermit crab

cow

horse

Farm animals
live in barns.

chickens

And some animals live in houses!

Animals That Live on Land

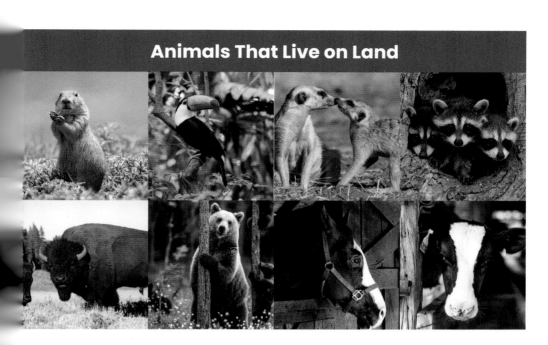

Animals That Live in Water

...READING REINFORCEMENT...

CONNECTING CONCEPTS

CLOSE READING OF NONFICTION TEXT

Close reading helps children comprehend text. It includes reading a text, discussing it with others, and answering questions about it. Use these questions to discuss this book with your child.

- What are four kinds of places where animals live?
- What is one animal that lives in a forest?
- Which kind of animal home is hot and dry?
- Where can you find coral reefs?
- What are two animals that build their own homes?

SCIENCE IN THE REAL WORLD

Have your child name a favorite animal that is not a type of pet. Talk about what you know about the animal and what it needs to survive. Ask your child to decide which page(s) the animal would be on if it was in this book. Then look at other books from the library or online to find more information about the animal.

SCIENCE AND ACADEMIC LANGUAGE

Make sure your child understands the meaning of the following words:

shelter	forest	desert	rocky	rain forest
prairie	fresh water	salty	water	coral reefs	shore

Have him or her use the words in a sentence.

FLUENCY

Fluency is the ability to read accurately with speed and expression. Help your child practice fluency by using one or more of the following activities:

1. Reread the book to your child at least two times while he or she uses a finger to track each word as it is read.

2. Read a line of the book, then reread it as your child reads along with you.

3. Ask your child to go back through the book and read the words he or she knows.

4. Have your child practice reading the book several times to improve accuracy, rate, and expression.

FOR FURTHER INFORMATION

Books:

Holland, Mary. *Animal Homes.* Mt. Pleasant: Arbordale Publishing, 2020.

Judge, Lita. *Homes in the Wild: Where Baby Animals and Their Parents Live.* New York: Roaring Brook Press, 2019.

Packham, Chris. *Amazing Animal Homes.* New York: Sterling Children's Books, 2018.

Websites:

PBS Learning Media: Habitat: Animal Homes
https://illinois.pbslearningmedia.org/resource/nat15.sci.lisci.anihome/habitat-animal-homes/#.YEuarC2cYW8

San Diego Zoo: Kids Corner: Animal Habitats
https://kids.sandiegozoo.org/videos/kids-corner-episode-2-animal-habitats

Time for Kids: Animal Homes
https://www.timeforkids.com/k1/animal-homes/

Word List

Where Animals Live uses the 95 words listed below. *High-frequency* words are those words that are used most often in the English language. They are sometimes referred to as sight words because children need to learn to recognize them automatically when they read. *Content* words are any words specific to a particular topic. Regular practice reading these words will enhance your child's ability to read with greater fluency and comprehension.

HIGH-FREQUENCY WORDS

a	each	home(s)	many	place(s)	these
all	few	house(s)	of	some	they
and	find	in	off	take(s)	to
are	for	is	on	the	water
around	from	it	only	their	where
can	give(s)	just	other(s)	them	work
different	have	like	own	there	

CONTENT WORDS

animal(s)	dry	keep	pads	sea
barns	falling	lakes	ponds	shelter
basketball	farm	land	prairie(s)	shoes
build	food	live	rain forest(s)	shore
climbing	forest	living	rainy	size
cold	fresh	months	reefs	summers
cool	full	mountain(s)	rivers	travel
coral	goat('s)	near	rocks	warm
dark	hooves	need(s)	rocky	winters
deep	hornets	nest	rough	world
desert	hot	ocean('s)	salty	

About the Author

Mary Lindeen is a writer, editor, parent, and former elementary school teacher. She has written more than 100 books for children and edited many more. She specializes in early literacy instruction and books for young readers, especially nonfiction.

About the Advisor

Dr. Shannon Cannon is an elementary school teacher in Sacramento, California. She has served as a teacher educator in the School of Education at UC Davis, where she also earned her PhD in Language, Literacy, and Culture. As a member of the clinical faculty, she supervised pre-service teachers and taught elementary methods courses in reading, effective teaching, and teacher action research.